WORD POWER

100 Words Every 3ʳᵈ GRADER Should Know

New York • Toronto • London • Auckland • Sydney
Mexico City • New Delhi • Hong Kong • Buenos Aires

Impress your friends!

AMAZING WORD POWER

Ace the tests!

Excel in School!

Delight your parents!

Welcome to Amazing Word Power!

By picking up this book you've entered the world of Amazing Words. And you're on your way to building your own Amazing Word Power.

There are 100 great words in this book. Some you may know already. Some may look familiar. But many of them are meant to challenge you! The illustrations and easy-to-understand definitions will help you to learn and remember them.

Ready? Before you get started, you may want to do the following:

1. Use the Checklist that starts on page 125 along with the back cover flap to see what words you know and don't know. (Be sure to use a dry-erase marker.) Do this again in a couple of weeks. This will help you keep track of your growing word power.

2. Check out the Word Power Tips on page 124. Following these tips will help you boost your word learning.

3. Learn more about the words. Many words have several definitions. We didn't include all these definitions, but you can find them—as well as information about the origins of the words—by looking in a dictionary or searching in an online dictionary.

4. Have fun!

Contents

account

(uh-**kount**) noun

What It Means

An arrangement to keep money in a bank, such as a savings or checking account

How to Use It

If you put $5 into your bank *account* each week, it will add up quickly.

More About It

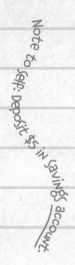 *Account* can also be used as a verb.

currency

(**kur**-uhn-see) noun

What It Means

The form of money used in a country

How to Use It

Currency in the U.S. shows the faces of famous Americans.

More About It

⊜ *Synonym*   money

The $20 bill is my favorite currency—but I don't have many of these bills!

3

frugal

(**froo**-guhl) adjective

What It Means

To be very careful
not to waste things

How to Use It

If you are really *frugal* with
your money, you can save
for fantastic things.

More About It

⇄ *Antonym*   wasteful

Mom says Dad is frugal. I say he's cheap!

splurge

(**splurj**) verb

What It Means

To buy something expensive that you probably don't need

How to Use It

Corey *splurged* and had a big sundae.

More About It

= *Synonym*   indulge

Yippee! Grandma splurged on a new bike for me.

bankrupt

(**bangk**-*ruhpt*) adjective

What It Means

Unable to pay back all the money you owe

How to Use It

The new restaurant quickly went *bankrupt*.

More About It

= *Synonym* broke

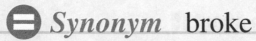

No money + lots of bills = bankrupt.

Activity Sheet

Read each clue. Then write the answers in the spiral puzzle. We did the first one for you.

1. Go nuts and buy something expensive that you don't really need.
2. You'd like to have a big fat one at the bank.
3. George Washington is on one, and Ben Franklin is, too.
4. A nicer way to say someone is really cheap!
5. All gone, broke
6. What this puzzle is all about
7. An antonym for *frugal*

E	2.		C		
G	5.				
R			T		3.
U	7.				
L		Y			
P				6.	
1. S		4.	Y		

START

6

malnutrition

(*mal*-noo-**trish**-uhn) _{noun}

I get it: mal means bad. Malnutrition is bad nutrition.

What It Means

A harmful condition caused by not having enough food or by eating the wrong kind of food

How to Use It

The lost dog had fleas and was suffering from *malnutrition.*

More About It

➤◄ *Related word*   malnourished

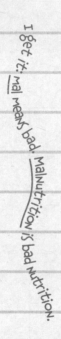

malicious

(muh-**lish**-uhss) adjective

What It Means

Intended to cause harm

How to Use It

Teasing me like that
is so *malicious*!

More About It

⇄ *Antonym*   kind

Malicious rhymes with vicious.

malfunction

(*mal*-**funk**-shuhn) noun

Boy, do I hate when we have a dishwasher malfunction.

What It Means

A breakdown or failure to function in the correct or normal way

How to Use It

There is a *malfunction* with the television.

More About It

= *Synonym*   breakdown

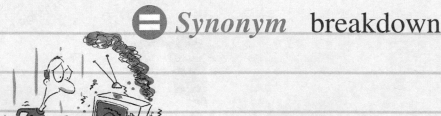

maltreatment

(*mal*-**treet**-muhnt) noun

What It Means

The cruel treatment of a person or animal

How to Use It

Rita will not tolerate the *maltreatment* of animals.

More About It

= *Synonym* abuse

Too much homework is student maltreatment!

10

malpractice

(*mal*-**prak**-tiss) noun

What It Means

The failure of a professional, like a doctor or a lawyer, to do his or her job responsibly

How to Use It

I thought you said the left leg...

The patient is suing the doctor for *malpractice*.

More About It

= *Synonym*   mismanagement

Malpractice = bad practice

Activity Sheet

Who said what? Draw a line from each kid on the left to the correct speech balloon on the right.

1. malnutrition

2. maltreatment

3. malpractice

4. malicious

5. malfunction

A. That was the meanest, most rotten thing you could have said to me!

B. He never showed his dog any love. And he didn't give it enough food.

C. Oops! I didn't know that my new pen would squirt all over you! There's something wrong with it.

D. On my camping trip, I ate nothing but berries and roots. I didn't get real food for three days.

E. The good news is that the doctor fixed my arm. The bad news is he fixed the wrong arm!

gargantuan

(gar-**gan**-*choo*-uhn) adjective

What It Means

To be very large in amount, number, or size

How to Use It

Wow! This is a *gargantuan* cucumber.

More About It

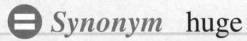 *Synonym* huge

I'd like to splurge on a gargantuan b-day party.

moderate

(**mod**-ur-it) adjective

Moderate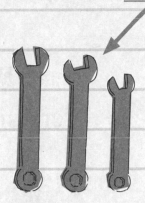

What It Means

Not extreme

How to Use It

Don't give me a wrench that's too big or too small. Give me one that's *moderate*.

More About It

⊜ *Synonym*   average

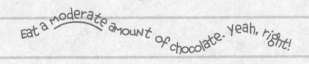

Eat a moderate amount of chocolate. Yeah, right!

puny

(**pyoo-nee**) adjective

What It Means

Very small or weak

How to Use It

Our team seemed *puny* compared to the other team.

More About It

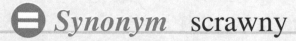 **≡** *Synonym*   scrawny

My bank account is puny. I need more $$$.

diminutive

(duh-**min**-yuh-tiv) adjective

I'm hoping for a diminutive amount of homework this weekend.

What It Means

Very small or tiny

How to Use It

Don't let his *diminutive* size fool you. He's the strongest person I know.

More About It

⇄ *Antonym* huge

Diminutive

15

hefty

(**hef-tee**) adjective

What It Means

Big and strong

How to Use It

That's a *hefty* load of books you're carrying. Do you need help?

More About It

hefty

⇄ *Antonym* tiny

A big cow is a hefty heifer. Ha ha!

Activity Sheet

Some new shops are opening up in town. They need help deciding on names. Read each description below. Then circle the name you think best fits the store.

1. A really huge car store

    Ⓐ Moderate Auto Mart   Ⓑ Gargantuan Garage

2. A very small store with lots and lots of things in it

    Ⓐ Diminutive But Packed   Ⓑ Hefty Clothes

3. A clothing store that doesn't have large or small sizes

    Ⓐ Moderate Clothes   Ⓑ Puny & Pretty

4. A store that only has very small things in it

    Ⓐ Puny 4 You   Ⓑ Gargantuan Galley

5. A sports store that sells equipment to get big and strong

    Ⓐ Diminutive Dave's   Ⓑ Hefty Hal's

perspective

(pur-**spek**-tiv) noun

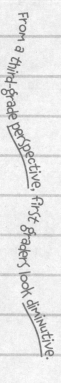

From a third-grade perspective, first graders look diminutive.

What It Means

A particular way of looking at or thinking about a situation

How to Use It

Astronauts have a great *perspective* of the Earth.

More About It

= *Synonym*　viewpoint

inspect

(in-**spekt**) verb

What It Means

To look at something
very carefully

How to Use It

The police officer *inspected*
the book for fingerprints.

More About It

⊜ *Synonym*   examine

I get it: Spect means look. Inspect means look in!

18

retrospective

(*re*-troh-**spek**-tiv) noun

3rd Grade Retrospective

What It Means

An exhibition of an artist's work done over a long period of time

How to Use It

There were more than 100 pieces of art in the "3rd Grade *Retrospective.*"

More About It

▶◀ *Related word* retrospect

Retro = back, so <u>retrospective</u> = look back.

spectator

(**spek**-tay-tur) noun

What It Means

Somebody who watches something, especially some kind of event

How to Use It

More *spectators* watch football than any other sport.

More About It

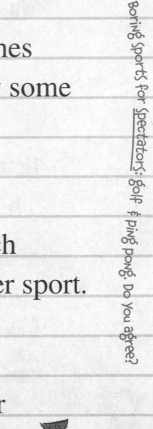

Boring sports for spectators: golf & ping pong. Do you agree?

⊜ *Synonym*   viewer

20

spectacle

(**spek**-tuh-kuhl) noun

What It Means

A remarkable or dramatic sight

How to Use It

The clown was quite a *spectacle*.

More About It

◀▶ *Related word*   spectacular

That robot malfunction was a hilarious spectacle.

Activity Sheet

What word can help you remember the meaning of the Latin root *spect*? Use the clues to fill in the correct words below. Then write the boxed letters at the bottom of the page.

1. A remarkable sight, such as fireworks or a parade
2. Someone who is watching an event
3. An exhibition of an artist's work
4. A particular way of thinking or seeing something
5. To examine something really carefully

1. _ _ _ _ _ _ □ _

2. _ _ _ _ _ □ _

3. _ _ _ □ _ _ _ _ _

4. _ _ _ _ _ _ _ □ _ _

5. _ □ _ _ _ _ _

_ _ _ K _ _ G
1 2 3   4 5

21

predator

(**pred**-uh-tur) noun

What It Means

An animal that hunts other animals for food

How to Use It

The shark is a fierce *predator*. Other fish stay away.

More About It

⇄ *Antonym* prey

Scariest predators: lions, Komodo dragons, and jackals. Yikes!

canine

(**kay**-nine) noun

What It Means

A dog or dog-like animal

How to Use It

The training school for *canines* works with all kinds of dogs.

More About It

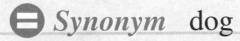 **Synonym**   dog

I ♥ my canine.

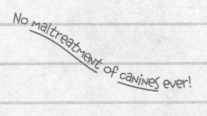
No maltreatment of canines ever!

feline

(**fee-line**) noun

What It Means

A cat or catlike animal

How to Use It

After our fourth kitten, Dad said, "No more *felines*!"

More About It

≡ *Synonym* cat

nocturnal

(nok-**tur**-nuhl) adjective

What It Means

Occurring at night, rather than during the day

How to Use It

The flying fox is a *nocturnal* animal. You'll never see it during the day.

More About It

= *Synonym*   nighttime

Are you kidding? I can't go to bed yet. I'm NOCTURNAL.

25

hibernate

(hye-bur-nate) verb

What It Means

When animals hibernate, they spend the winter in a deep sleep.

How to Use It

Bears *hibernate* all winter.

More About It

Hibernate comes from the Latin word *hibernus*, meaning "wintry."

Brr! It's too cold. Let's hibernate until spring.

Zzzzzz

Activity Sheet

Which of the critters below hibernates the longest? To find the answer, put an X in any space that contains two words that are synonyms. Then find a path formed by the spaces with an X. You can move up, down, right, left, or diagonally. The path will lead you to the answer. Some words come from earlier sections of this book.

START

hibernate sleep	puny hefty	gargantuan diminutive	bankrupt wealthy	puny strong
frugal cheap	predator hunter	inspect insect	feline dog	canine cat
malicious delicious	dog canine	moderate large	nocturnal nighttime	currency money
spectator respect	feline cat	malfunction breakdown	predator meat-eater	nocturnal daytime
bankrupt interrupt	splurge save	malicious good	gargantuan tiny	prey predator

bear

alligator

ground squirrel

raccoon

fox

26 villain

(vil-uhn) noun

Red Riding Hood = hero. Big Bad wolf = villain.

What It Means

Someone who hurts people on purpose, or breaks the law to get what he or she wants

How to Use It

The actor was good at playing the *villain*. Everyone hated him.

villain

More About It

= *Synonym*   rogue

despicable

(di-**spik**-uh-buhl) adjective

What It Means

Extremely nasty, cruel, or evil

How to Use It

Someone who steals food from the poor is really *despicable*.

With this new potion, I'll control the world's ice-cream supply! I love being despicable! Mwah-ha-ha!

More About It

⇄ *Antonym*   lovable

heroic

(hi-**roh**-ik) adjective

What It Means

Very brave or daring

How to Use It

Dash admired the *heroic* soldier.

More About It

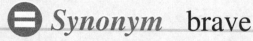 **Synonym** brave

Does taking out the trash in the rain count as heroic?

noble

(**noh**-buhl) adjective

What It Means

Idealistic and
considerate

Saving <u>felines</u>: noble.
Saving <u>canines</u>: noble.
Saving rats: Not So <u>noble</u>.

How to Use It

You can always count on
Tito to do the *noble* thing.

More About It

⊜ *Synonym*   honorable

Let me help
you with this.

Geez, you're
So <u>noble</u>.

scoundrel

(**skoun**-druhl) noun

What It Means

A person who behaves badly toward other people, especially by cheating or lying

He copied. He stole. He lied. What a scoundrel!

How to Use It

Don't let that *scoundrel* cheat us at cards again.

More About It

= *Synonym* villain

Activity Sheet

Read each clue. Then write the answers in the spiral puzzle.

1. Idealistic and considerate
2. Nasty, cruel, or evil
3. Very brave or daring
4. A person who behaves badly
5. The bad person in a movie
6. An antonym for *despicable*
7. A synonym for *villain*

		P				
2.			**5.**			
				7.		
						3.
B				**G**		
		V		**6.**		**R**
1.			**4.**			

START

testament

(**tess**-tuh-muhnt) noun

What It Means

Something that shows
what you believe

How to Use It

This list of rules is a *testament*
to how strict you are!

More About It

= *Synonym*   testimony

My testament: Be noble. Never be malicious.

testify

(**tess**-tuh-fye) verb

What It Means

To state the truth, or to give evidence in court

How to Use It

Molly had to *testify* against her own neighbor in court.

More About It

 *Antonym*   disprove

My brother caN <u>testify</u> about my Need for curreNcy.

detest

(di-**test**) verb

I detest tests.

What It Means

To dislike somebody or something very much

How to Use It

Nina *detests* the color green.

More About It

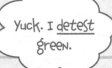 *Synonym*   despise

Yuck. I <u>detest</u> green.

attest

(uh-**test**) verb

What It Means

To show that something exists or is true or valid

How to Use It

Yes, I can *attest* to the fact that it is colder today than yesterday.

More About It

= *Synonym* swear

My room is not always clean. My mom will <u>attest</u> to that.

35

testimony

(**tess**-tuh-*moh*-nee) noun

Give your testimony in the microphon-y. LOL!

What It Means

A statement that a witness gives in a court of law

How to Use It

Her *testimony* convinced the jury to find her not guilty.

More About It

 *Related word* testimonial

Activity Sheet

Use the clues to fill in the correct words below. Then write the boxed letters on the lines below to name an important person at a trial. This word is also one of the meanings of the Latin root *test*.

1. To give evidence in court
2. To really dislike something
3. Something that shows what you believe
4. To show that something is true or valid
5. A statement given in court
6. A synonym for *detest*

1. _ _ _ _ ☐ _ _

2. _ _ ☐ _ _ _

3. _ _ _ _ _ _ ☐ _

4. _ _ _ ☐ _ _

5. _ _ ☐ _ _ _ _ _

6. _ _ ☐ _ _ _ _

W _ _ _ _ _
1 2 3 4 5 6

assert

(uh-**surt**) verb

What It Means

To state something as being true

How to Use It

Keisha often *asserts* her opinion as class president.

More About It

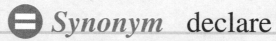 *Synonym*   declare

I assert that you should speak up.

utter

(**uht-ur**) verb

What It Means

To speak or make a sound from your mouth

How to Use It

My baby sister was able to *utter* the entire alphabet before she could walk.

More About It

⊜ *Synonym*   speak

I won't utter a word to that villain! He is despicable! Plain and Simple.

38 reiterate

(**ree**-it-ur-ate) verb

What It Means

To say something again, usually to emphasize it

How to Use It

The poet *reiterated* the title of her poem.

More About It

The Tree.
The Tree.

⊜ *Synonym*   repeat

My mom likes to reiterate, "Let me reiterate."

rebuke

(ri-**byook**) verb

What It Means

To scold or admonish someone because he or she has done something wrong

How to Use It

My mom *rebuked* me for breaking the window.

More About It

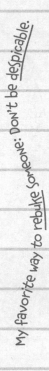

My favorite way to rebuke someone: Don't be despicable.

= *Synonym* scold

I told you not to play near a window.

candid

(**kan**-did) adjective

I'm always candid with my friends.

What It Means

Honest and open

How to Use It

Thomas was *candid* about not doing his homework.

More About It

 Synonym straightforward

I must be candid. I didn't do my math, my spelling, my science . . .

Activity Sheet

Play the game of Out and Over. Find a word in Box 1 that does not have the same meaning as the other three words. Move that word to Box 2 by writing it on the blank line. Continue until you reach Box 8. Then complete the sentence in that box.

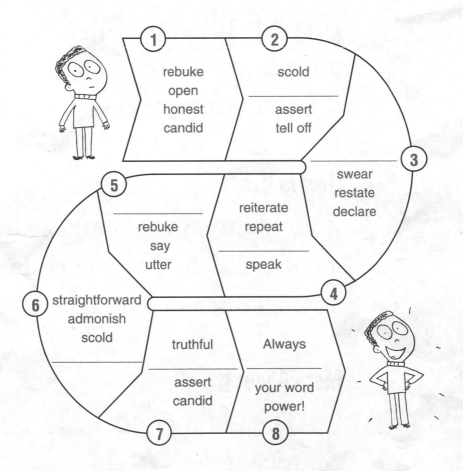

1
rebuke
open
honest
candid

2
scold
_____
assert
tell off

3
_____
swear
restate
declare

4

5
_____
rebuke
say
utter

reiterate
repeat
_____
speak

6 straightforward
admonish
scold

truthful
_____
assert
candid

Always
_____
your word
power!

7

8

decathlon

(di-**kath**-lon) noun

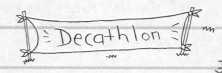

What It Means

A competition in which athletes compete in ten different track events

How to Use It

Can you imagine being such a good athlete that you could compete in a *decathlon*?

More About It

The Latin prefix *dec-* means "ten."

My decathlon: eating, sleeping, drawing, singing, texting, eating, playing, laughing, IMing, eating.

marathon

(**mar**-uh-thon) noun

Run a marathon? 26 miles! Forget it!

What It Means

A long-distance footrace; a test of endurance, especially in a competition

How to Use It

Thousands of people run in the New York City *marathon* each year.

More About It

💬 *Marathon* was the name of a town where the Greeks won a battle.

hurdle

(**hur**-duhl) noun

What It Means

A small fence that you jump over in a running event

How to Use It

She jumped over the four *hurdles* easily.

More About It

➤➤ *Related word* hurdler

Note to Self: Hurdle too high. Get longer legs!

torch

(torch) noun

What It Means

A flaming light that can be carried by hand

How to Use It

It is cool that they keep the Olympic *torch* lit all year.

More About It

In England, people use the word *torch* to mean "flashlight."

The Statue of Liberty holds a torch.

ceremony

(**ser**-uh-*moh*-nee) noun

What It Means

Formal actions, words, and often music performed to mark an important occasion

How to Use It

The Olympics *ceremony* includes a parade.

More About It

⊜ *Synonym* ritual

My aunt Lori's wedding ceremony was fun!

Activity Sheet

Can you win the gold? Find the finish line on the right that includes words that tell about each runner's word. Then draw a line from the runner to the correct finish line.

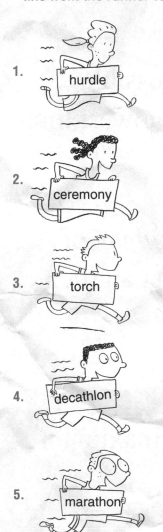

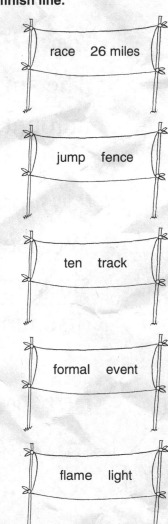

1. hurdle

A.   race   26 miles

2. ceremony

B.   jump   fence

3. torch

C.   ten   track

4. decathlon

D.   formal   event

5. marathon

E.   flame   light

46

minimum

(**min**-uh-muhm) noun

What It Means

The smallest possible amount, or the lowest limit

How to Use It

We need a *minimum* of six people to get a group discount.

My sister needs 30 minutes MINIMUM to do her hair.

More About It

⇄ *Antonym*   maximum

horde

(**hord**) noun

What It Means

A large, noisy group of people or animals

How to Use It

A *horde* of angry people yelled when the movie was over.

More About It

= *Synonym*   crowd

My dad calls us kids a <u>horde</u> of scoundrels.

48

paltry

(**pawl-tree**) adjective

What It Means

Small, worthless, or unimportant

How to Use It

This *paltry* serving is my lunch?!

More About It

⊜ *Synonym*   insignificant

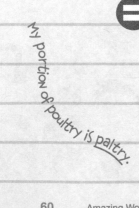

My portion of poultry is paltry.

maximum

(**mak**-suh-muhm) noun

What It Means

The largest possible amount, or the upper limit

That taxi exceeds the monkey maximum!

How to Use It

My mom said three kids was the *maximum* I could have at my sleep over.

More About It

 *Antonym*   minimum

abundance

(uh-**buhn**-duhnss) noun

I'd like an abundance of currency.

What It Means

A very large quantity of something

How to Use It

Wow! This is an *abundance* of ice cream.

More About It

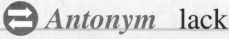 *Antonym* lack

Activity Sheet

It's silly riddle time. Complete each silly riddle using one of the words in the box below.

abundance	maximum	minimum	horde	paltry

1. What do you call a big group of people with nothing to do?

   a bored _____

2. What do you call a big bag full of hamburger buns?

   _____

3. What did people call Paul's tiny tree?

   _____

4. Why did the little old lady live in a shoe?

   There was only room for a:

   _____

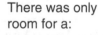

5. Why was Max's mother the last one allowed in the elevator?

   The elevator had reached the

   _____

51

overwhelm

(*oh*-vur-**welm**) verb

Memorize all the state capitals?! That will overwhelm me.

What It Means

To defeat or to have a very strong effect

How to Use It

Paperwork *overwhelmed* the bookkeeper.

More About It

= *Synonym*   overcome

appalling

(uh-**paw**-ling) adjective

Gross! Yech! Despicable! Yep, it's appalling.

What It Means

Horrifying or shocking

How to Use It

My parents find my messy room *appalling*.

More About It

⊜ *Synonym*　upsetting

intimidate

(in-**tim**-uh-*dayt*) verb

What It Means

To make someone afraid or to frighten someone

How to Use It

Bugs completely *intimidate* my mother.

More About It

= *Synonym*   frighten

Talk about intimidating! check out word 21.

elated

(i-**lay**-tid) adjective

What It Means

Pleased and excited about something

How to Use It

I was *elated* when our team won.

More About It

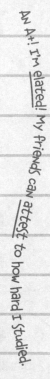

⇄ *Antonym*   sad

An A+! I'm elated! My friends can attest to how hard I studied.

grateful

(**grayt**-fuhl) adjective

What It Means

Appreciative and thankful for something

How to Use It

My father was *grateful* the storm didn't damage our house.

More About It

 *Related word* gratitude

Don't be hateful. Be grateful.

Activity Sheet

Are you "feeling" up to making some matches? Draw a line from each kid on the left to the speech balloon that tells how he or she is feeling.

1. Overwhelmed Olly

A.

I am shocked and disgusted by your behavior!

2. Appalled Ally

B.

Thank you. I really appreciate it.

3. Intimidated Izzy

C.

Stop. It's too much. I can't do anymore.

4. Elated Eddy

D.

I'm nervous about this. It seems too scary.

5. Grateful Gabby

E.

I am so totally thrilled to be here!

scorching

(**skor**-ching) adjective

What It Means

Very, very hot

How to Use It

I am melting in this *scorching* heat!

More About It

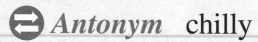 *Antonym*   chilly

Florida in July? Scorching!

tropical

(**trop**-uh-kuhl) adjective

What It Means

To be like the hot
and steamy tropics

How to Use It

On my *tropical* vacation, I
climbed trees in the rain forest.

More About It

 *Related word* tropics

Let's be <u>candid</u>. <u>Tropical</u> vacations sizzle!

temperate

(**tem**-pur-it) adjective

What It Means

A climate that is neither too hot nor too cold

How to Use It

The *temperate* weather was just right for a picnic.

More About It

≡ *Synonym*   pleasant

Goldilocks gobbled all the temperate porridge. Gross.

torrent

(tor-uhnt) noun

Boo-hoo! Boo-hoo! Boo-hoo! (A torrent of tears.)

What It Means

A fast, violent rush of liquid, usually water

How to Use It

The *torrent* of rain made it impossible for cars to drive.

More About It

≡ *Synonym* downpour

frigid

(**frij-id**) adjective

What It Means

Very, very cold

How to Use It

Are you crazy!? You need to wear a coat in this *frigid* weather.

More About It

 Antonym sweltering

I'd rather the weather be scorching than frigid.

Activity Sheet

Use the comments below about the weather to complete the puzzle.

ACROSS

1. With this _____ of rain, my umbrella isn't even helping.

4. I feel faint. I'm dehydrated. I'm getting sunburned!

DOWN

1. Yes, I'll have another fresh coconut, please. Then I'm going into the ocean.

2. It's not too hot today. Nor is it too cold. You know what? It's perfect!

3. Brr! I should have worn a heavier jacket.

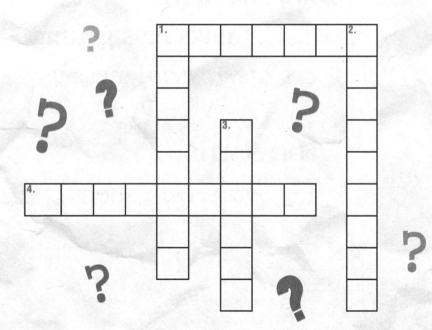

extraterrestrial

(*ek*-struh-tuh-**ress**-tree-uhl) adjective

What It Means

Coming from outer space

How to Use It

T. C. thinks he's getting *extraterrestrial* messages.

More About It

= *Synonym*   alien

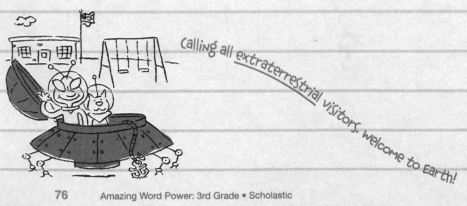

Calling all extraterrestrial visitors, welcome to Earth!

extraordinary

(ek-**stror**-duh-*ner*-ee) adjective

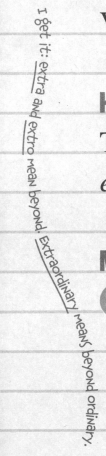

I get it: extra and extro mean beyond. Extraordinary means beyond ordinary.

What It Means

Very unusual

How to Use It

The superhero had *extraordinary* strength!

More About It

= *Synonym*   special

extracurricular

(**ek**-struh-kuh-**rik**-yuh-lur) adjective

What It Means

Outside of school

How to Use It

Josie participates in two *extracurricular* activities.

> I think I need a new extracurricular activity. Ouch! Ouch! Ouch!

More About It

 *Antonym*   curricular

> Tee-hee-hee.

extravagant

(ek-**strav**-uh-guhnt) adjective

What It Means

Wasteful, or very high in price or cost

How to Use It

My aunt Ruby gives me *extravagant* gifts.

More About It

 **Antonym** frugal

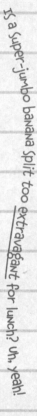

Is a super-jumbo banana split too extravagant for lunch? Uh, yeah!

extrovert

(ek-struh-vurt) noun

What It Means

Someone who enjoys being with other people and is lively and talkative

How to Use It

J. Z. is an *extrovert*. He'll talk whenever he can.

More About It

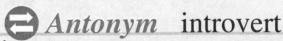 *Antonym*   introvert

Everyone knows I'm an extrovert. I ♥ talking (a lot).

Activity Sheet

Clues to words with the Latin prefix *extra/extro* are in the news! Look at the headlines below. Match each one to the correct newspaper seller on the left.

1. Extrovert!

A. **The Post** — Alien From Space Lands in Iowa

2. Extraterrestrial!

B. **The Post** — Farmer Wins Prize for Very Unusual Plant

3. Extravagant!

C. **The Post** — Lively and Talkative Person Needed for Job

4. Extracurricular!

D. **The Post** — Very Expensive Gift Given to Family

5. Extraordinary!

E. **The Post** — More After-School Activities Needed

66

compassionate

(kuhm-**pash**-uh-nit) adjective

Be compassionate: Donate toys and clothes.

What It Means

A feeling of sympathy for others and a desire to help those who are suffering

How to Use It

Eduardo is very *compassionate* and likes to volunteer at the hospital.

I'M compassionate. I like helping people.

More About It

= *Synonym* sympathetic

yeah, but he's not humble.

amiable

(**ay**-mee-uh-buhl) adjective

What It Means

Friendly and pleasant
to be with

How to Use It

Our *amiable* neighbors
always say hello to us.

More About It

⇌ *Antonym* unfriendly

Amiable teachers: assert yourselves and give less homework tonight!

glum

(**gluhm**) adjective

What It Means

Sad and miserable

How to Use It

I've never seen Tony so *glum* before.

More About It

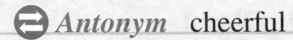 *Antonym* cheerful

You know what makes me glum? Look at word 59.

feisty

(fye-stee) adjective

What It Means

Easily angered or likely to quarrel

How to Use It

My dog can be surprisingly *feisty*.

Dry food again!

More About It

⇄ *Antonym*   calm

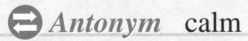

Let me reiterate: My little brother is definitely feisty.

versatile

(**vur**-suh-tuhl) adjective

What It Means

Talented or useful in
many ways

How to Use It

The seal was very *versatile*.

More About It

⊜ *Synonym*   adaptable

My goals: Be versatile. Be amiable.

Activity Sheet

Play the game of Out and Over. Find a word in Box 1 that does not have the same meaning as the other three words. Move that word to Box 2 by writing it on the blank line. Continue until you reach Box 8. Then complete the sentence in that box.

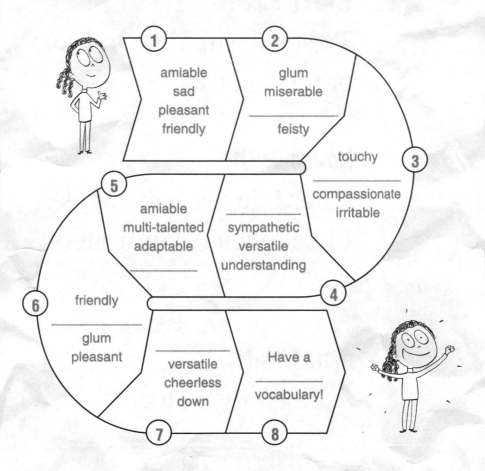

1
amiable
sad
pleasant
friendly

2
glum
miserable
_____
feisty

3
touchy
_____
compassionate
irritable

4
_____
sympathetic
versatile
understanding

5
amiable
multi-talented
adaptable
_____

6
friendly
_____
glum
pleasant

7
_____
versatile
cheerless
down

8
Have a
_____
vocabulary!

lounge

(lounj) verb

What It Means

To stand, sit, or lie in a lazy or relaxed way

How to Use It

After I do my homework, I like to *lounge* in front of the TV.

Lounging is one of my favorite activities.

More About It

= *Synonym*   loaf

slumber

(**sluhm**-bur) verb

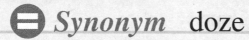

Saturday morning is my time to <u>slumber</u>.

What It Means

To sleep

How to Use It

Some people snore when they *slumber*.

More About It

═ *Synonym* doze

enhance

(en-**hanss**) verb

What It Means

To make something
better or greater

How to Use It

The chef *enhanced* the recipe
by adding chocolate chips.

More About It

= *Synonym* improve

Chocolate chips enhance everything!

frolic

(**frol**-ik) verb

What It Means

To play happily

How to Use It

Kimmi loves to *frolic* in the park.

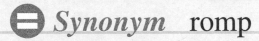

My dog loves to frolic in the snow.

More About It

= Synonym romp

75

immerse

(i-**murss**) verb

My dad and I like to immerse ourselves in watching football.

What It Means

To involve yourself in something completely

How to Use It

Sometimes I like to *immerse* myself in a good book.

More About It

⊜ *Synonym*   engross

Activity Sheet

What's your favorite thing to do on a Saturday morning? Keep choosing between pairs to find out! Write your choice for each pair in the box to the right until you get to the last box. Some of the words come from earlier sections of this book.

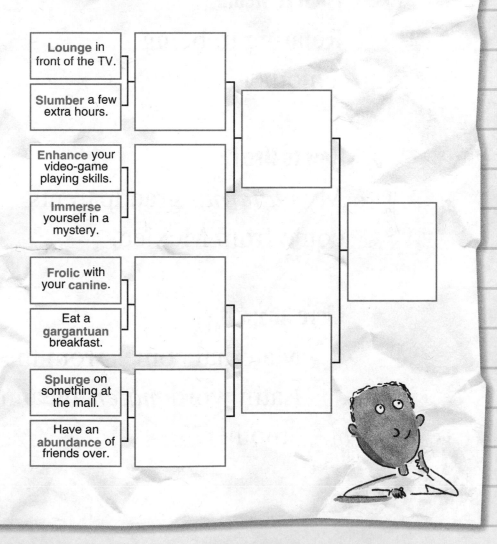

Lounge in front of the TV.

Slumber a few extra hours.

Enhance your video-game playing skills.

Immerse yourself in a mystery.

Frolic with your **canine**.

Eat a **gargantuan** breakfast.

Splurge on something at the mall.

Have an **abundance** of friends over.

maternal

(muh-**tur**-nuhl) adjective

Lucky for me, my mom is very maternal.

What It Means

Relating to being a mother

How to Use It

My *maternal* grandparents come from Mexico.

More About It

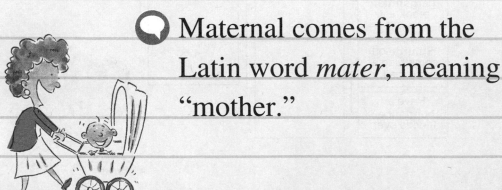

Maternal comes from the Latin word *mater*, meaning "mother."

paternal

(puh-**tur**-nuhl) adjective

What It Means

Relating to being
a father

How to Use It

My *paternal* grandparents
come from Cuba.

More About It

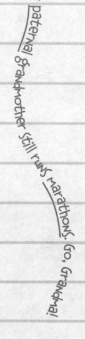

My paternal grandmother still runs marathons. Go, Grandma!

Paternal comes from
the Latin word *pater*,
meaning "father."

sibling

(sib-ling) noun

My sibling is just a baby. She's so cute!

What It Means

A brother or sister

How to Use It

I have three *siblings*—one sister and twin brothers.

More About It

Sibling comes from an Old English word meaning "relative."

offspring

(**of**-*spring*) noun

What It Means

The descendants of people, animals, or sometimes plants

How to Use It

My dog has many *offspring*.

More About It

= *Synonym* descendant

yikes! My maternal grandfather has 22 offspring!

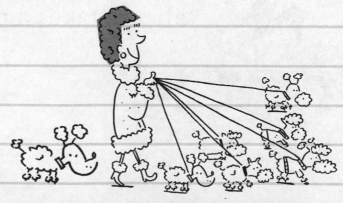

kin

(**kin**) noun

Some of my <u>kin</u> live 1000 miles away!

What It Means

The people related to you

How to Use It

All of Hector's *kin* get together at least once a year.

More About It

 *Kin* is a plural noun, so it always takes a plural verb.

Activity Sheet

Use the words you learned about family members to answer these brain teasers. Then answer the Super-Tricky Brain Teaser at the bottom of the page.

1. She's your maternal grandmother's daughter. She could be your
   <u>A</u> ____ ____ ____ or your ____ ____ ____ ____ ____.
        ₁

2. Your sister is not your cousin. Your cousin is not your sister. They
   both, however, are your ____ ____ ____.
               ₂

3. He's your paternal grandparent's son. He could be your
   <u>U</u> ____ ____ ____ ____ or your ____ ____ ____ ____ ____.
        ₃

4. This animal likes to slumber in the sun and chase a mouse or
   two. Its offspring are called ____ ____ ____ ____ ____ ____ ____.
            ₄

Now try this Super-Tricky Brain Teaser. To check your answer, put each numbered letter from above on the blank with the same number.

Nick's mother has three sons. The oldest sibling is named Red. The middle sibling is named White. What is the youngest sibling's name?

____ ____ ____ ____
1   2   3   4

scurry

(**skur-ee**) verb

Personally, I never scurry. But I do frolic.

What It Means

To move quickly because you are frightened

How to Use It

The sheep *scurried* away when it heard the loud noise.

More About It

= *Synonym* scamper

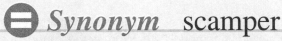

rummage

(**ruhm**-ij) verb

I spend too much time rummaging through my backpack.

What It Means

To make a quick search through something

How to Use It

Josh *rummaged* through the old trunk.

More About It

= *Synonym*   search

trudge

(**truhj**) verb

What It Means

To walk slowly and with heavy steps because you are tired or sick

How to Use It

The climbers *trudged* up the mountain.

More About It

 *Synonym* plod

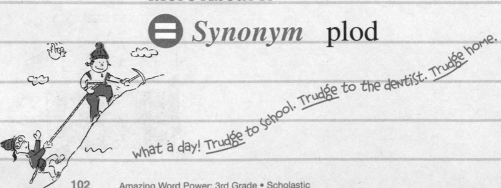

What a day! Trudge to school. Trudge to the dentist. Trudge home.

linger

(ling-gur) verb

What It Means

To stay or wait around

How to Use It

I usually *linger* after my basketball game to practice my jump shots.

More About It

⊜ *Synonym*   remain

I think I'll linger here for a while.

I like to linger in front of the TV.

START

lurch

(lurch) verb

What It Means

To move in an unsteady, jerky way

How to Use It

The bear *lurched* toward the beehive.

My baby sister doesn't walk. She lurches!

More About It

= *Synonym*   stagger

watch out! This bike makes me lurch!

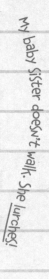

Activity Sheet

What runs but cannot walk? Write the correct word for each clue. Then write the boxed letters on the lines at the bottom of the page to answer the riddle.

1. To move quickly because you are scared
2. To walk slowly, with heavy steps
3. A synonym for *stagger*
4. To stay or wait around
5. A synonym for *search*

1. ☐ _ _ _ _ _

2. ☐ _ _ _ _ _

3. _ _ ☐ _ _ _

4. _ _ _ _ ☐ _

5. _ _ _ _ ☐ _ _

A _ _ _ _ _ M
   1 2 3 4 5

franchise

(**fran**-chize) noun

Check out word 5. That's what can happen when you spend too much time in franchises!

What It Means

Permission given by a company to sell its services or distribute its products in a certain area

How to Use It

I like a mall that has my favorite *franchises* in it.

More About It

Franchise also refers to the right to vote.

inventory

(**in**-vuhn-*tor*-ee) noun

What It Means

A complete list of items someone owns; all the items available for sale in a store

How to Use It

Once they counted everything in the store, they had a sale on all *inventory*.

More About It

💬 *Inventory* can also be used as a verb.

My backpack inventory:
4 books
1 cell phone
3 pencils
2 pens
2 notebooks
1 smashed sandwich

receipt

(ri-**seet**) noun

I shop a lot. I have an abundance of receipts to prove it.

What It Means

Written or printed proof that you paid for something

How to Use It

Keep the *receipt* in case you want to return the sneakers.

receipt

More About It

💬 Be sure you don't pronounce the *p* in *receipt*. It is silent.

supervisor

(**soo**-pur-*vye*-zur) noun

What It Means

Somebody whose job is to oversee the work of other people

How to Use It

Oops! She is my *supervisor*. I don't want her to see me goofing off.

More About It

 = *Synonym*   boss

 Hey! I'm the Supervisor here!

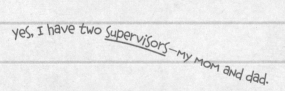 yes, I have two Supervisors—my mom and dad.

transaction

(tran-**zak**-shuhn) noun

A frigid transaction? Money for ice cream.

I use currency for all my transactions.

What It Means

An exchange of goods, services, or money

How to Use It

It took 20 minutes for the cashier to ring up the customer. That was a LONG *transaction*.

More About It

= *Synonym*   deal

Activity Sheet

Use the clues to complete the puzzle.

ACROSS

2. A synonym for *boss*

6. An exchange of something (goods, services, or money)

7. A list of items that someone owns

8. Your mom might say, "Don't _____ all your money!"

DOWN

1. 99 cents plus 1 cent equals one of these.

3. Don't forget this when you are returning items to a store.

4. A store or restaurant controlled by a parent company

5. Another word for *shop*

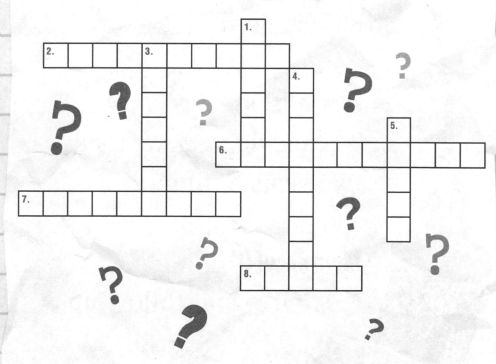

sequel

(**see**-kwuhl) noun

Harry rocks! I'm elated with the final Harry Potter sequel.

What It Means

A book or movie that continues the story of an earlier work

How to Use It

The movie's *sequel* took two years to film.

More About It

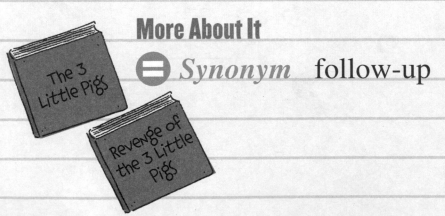

⊜ *Synonym* follow-up

The 3 Little Pigs

Revenge of the 3 Little Pigs

saga

(**sah**-guh) noun

What It Means

A long story or series of stories, often following the lives of a family over several generations

Sagas go on . . . and on . . . and on . . . and on . . . and on . . . and on . . .

How to Use It

My favorite movie *saga* is *Star Wars*.

More About It

💬 *Saga* means "story" in Old Norse, a language spoken long ago in Norway and Iceland.

rousing

(**rou**-zing) adjective

I hope we have a rousing school assembly today.

What It Means

Attention-getting or exciting

How to Use It

Newspapers use *rousing* headlines to catch people's attention.

More About It

⊜ *Synonym* lively

epic

(ep-ik) noun

What It Means

A long story, poem, or movie about heroic adventures and great battles

How to Use It

It takes many years to film an *epic* like *Lord of the Rings*.

More About It

💬 *Epic* comes from a Greek word meaning "speech."

Have a seat. This <u>epic</u> is long.

My life story would be quite an <u>epic</u>.

marquee

(mar-**kee**) noun

Favorite marquee: "Kids Free Today."

What It Means

A large awning over a theater entrance that displays the name of the play or movie

How to Use It

The movie *marquee* read, "Dancing Dogs."

More About It

= *Synonym* canopy

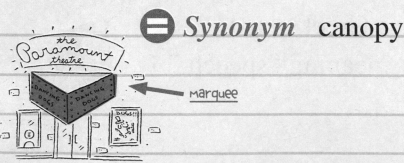

the Paramount theatre

DANCING DOGS DANCING DOGS

DOGS!!

marquee

Activity Sheet

It's a movie-time match-up. Find the popcorn bucket on the right that includes the correct definition of the word on the left. Then draw a line from the word to the bucket.

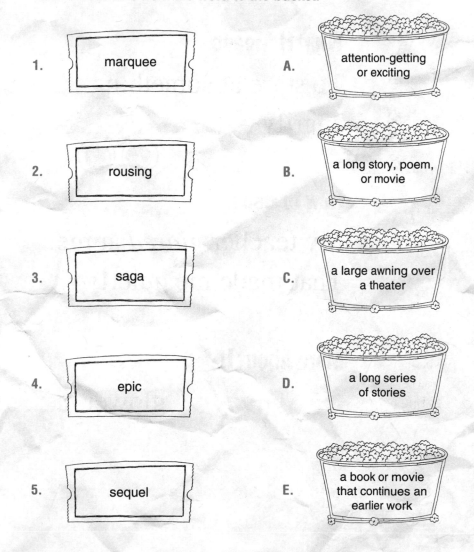

1. marquee

2. rousing

3. saga

4. epic

5. sequel

A. attention-getting or exciting

B. a long story, poem, or movie

C. a large awning over a theater

D. a long series of stories

E. a book or movie that continues an earlier work

glare

(**glair**) verb

glare = To stare in a way that scares.

What It Means

To stare at something angrily

How to Use It

My teacher *glared* at me. That made me quiet!

More About It

Uh, oh. You're glaring.

= *Synonym*   glower

glimpse

(glimps) verb

What It Means

To get a quick or incomplete look at something

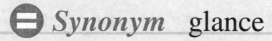

I like to glimpse the endings of books.

How to Use It

The bus went by so fast, I barely *glimpsed* it.

More About It

⊜ *Synonym*   glance

I was hoping to glimpse the park.

I glimpse money in my future!

scrutinize

(**skroot**-uh-*nize*) verb

What It Means

To examine something or somebody very carefully

How to Use It

The doctor *scrutinized* the X-ray very carefully.

More About It

⊜ *Synonym*　inspect

Hey! Scrutinize word 17. Notice anything?

scan

(**skan**) verb

What It Means

To read or look through something quickly

How to Use It

Jessica likes to *scan* the newspaper every morning.

More About It

⊜ *Synonym* skim

Did you *scan* the invite list? AM I ON it? AM I? AM I?

gaze

(**gayz**) verb

With such an extraordinary vocabulary, people will gaze at me in wonder!

What It Means

To look at something for a long time

How to Use It

Astronomers *gaze* at the stars and planets.

More About It

= *Synonym*   stare

Activity Sheet

Read each clue. Then write the answers in the spiral puzzle.

1. To stare at something angrily
2. To get a quick or incomplete look at something
3. To inspect carefully
4. A synonym for *skim*
5. To look at something for a long time
6. A synonym for *glare*
7. A synonym for *scrutinize*
8. A synonym for *glimpse*

					3. E
2.			6.		
		T	8.		
5.					
			N		
	A			7.	
1.		4.			N

START

Word Power Tips

Are you ready to add 100 words to your vocabulary? Check out the 10 tips below. They're a great way to help boost your Amazing Word Power!

1. **Keep Track of Your Progress.** Use the Checklist that starts on page 125 with the back cover flap to keep track of your growing vocabulary. Cover the definitions with the flap and quiz yourself. (Be sure to use a dry-erase marker.) Test yourself every few weeks to see how many new words you have learned.

2. **Say the Word Aloud.** A pronunciation is given for every word, and you'll also find a pronunciation guide on the inside of the back cover flap. Saying the word will help you remember it better. And the more you say it, the better chance you have of remembering it!

3. **Look at the Illustrations.** Some people remember better when they see a picture, so be sure you look at the illustration included for each word. The illustration may be the key to helping you remember the word's meaning.

4. **Read Each Section of the Word Page.** The more times you encounter a word, the more likely you are to remember it. Each page is designed to give you lots of opportunities to see the word and understand how it is used. The More About It sections include additional information about the words (see the key on the inside back cover flap).

5. **Think About the Word Groups.** How are the words in each group related? Do they share a Latin or Greek root? Are they all ways to describe something? If you can remember what group a word is in, it will help you figure out its meaning the next time you see it.

6. **Do the Activity.** At the end of each group of words, there is an activity page. Doing the activity will help you use and remember the words. Plus, they're fun!

7. **Write Your Own Sentence.** It's true: Using a new word in a sentence helps you to remember it. Try writing your own sentence for each word.

8. **Listen for the Words.** See how often these words come up in conversations, in school, on TV, or in movies.

9. **Look for the Words.** Look for these words online or as you're reading your favorite books or magazines. Make it a game to find them as often as possible.

10. **Use the Words Whenever You Can.** Don't be afraid to exercise your word power! Use your new words as much as you can when you are speaking and writing. You'll amaze your friends, your parents, and your teachers!

1.	account	account: a place to save money in a bank
2.	currency	currency: a country's form of money
3.	frugal	frugal: very careful not to waste things
4.	splurge	splurge: to buy something expensive
5.	bankrupt	bankrupt: unable to pay money you owe
6.	malnutrition	malnutrition: not having enough food
7.	malicious	malicious: intended to cause harm
8.	malfunction	malfunction: a breakdown or failure
9.	maltreatment	maltreatment: bad treatment
10.	malpractice	malpractice: failure of a professional to do a good job
11.	gargantuan	gargantuan: large in amount, number, or size
12.	moderate	moderate: not extreme
13.	puny	puny: very weak or small
14.	diminutive	diminutive: very small or tiny
15.	hefty	hefty: big and strong
16.	perspective	perspective: a particular way of seeing something
17.	inspect	inspect: to look at something closely
18.	retrospective	retrospective: an artist's exhibition
19.	spectator	spectator: somebody who watches something
20.	spectacle	spectacle: a remarkable sight
21.	predator	predator: an animal that hunts other animals for food
22.	canine	canine: a dog
23.	feline	feline: a cat
24.	nocturnal	nocturnal: occurring at night
25.	hibernate	hibernate: to sleep during the winter
26.	villain	villain: a person who hurts others on purpose
27.	despicable	despicable: extremely nasty or cruel
28.	heroic	heroic: very brave or daring
29.	noble	noble: idealistic and considerate
30.	scoundrel	scoundrel: a person who lies and cheats
31.	testament	testament: something that shows what you believe
32.	testify	testify: to state the truth
33.	detest	detest: to dislike someone very much

(Continued on page 127)

Answer Key

Page 9
1. splurge
2. account
3. currency
4. frugal
5. bankrupt
6. money
7. wasteful

Page 15
1. D
2. B
3. E
4. A
5. C

Page 21
1. B
2. A
3. A
4. A
5. B

Page 27
1. spectacle
2. spectator
3. retrospective
4. perspective
5. inspect
LOOKING

Page 33
An adult ground squirrel may hibernate for 7 to 9 months.

Page 39
1. noble
2. despicable
3. heroic
4. scoundrel
5. villain
6. lovable
7. rogue

Page 45
1. testify
2. detest
3. testament

4. attest
5. testimony
6. despise
WITNESS

Page 51
Words that move out are:
1. rebuke
2. assert
3. restate
4. speak
5. rebuke
6. straightforward
7. assert

Page 57
1. B
2. D
3. E
4. C
5. A

Page 63
1. horde
2. abundance
3. paltry
4. minimum
5. maximum

Page 69
1. C
2. A
3. D
4. E
5. B

Page 75
Across
1. torrent
4. scorching
Down
1. tropical
2. temperate
3. frigid

Page 81
1. C
2. A
3. D
4. E
5. B

Page 87
Words that move out are:
1. sad
2. feisty
3. compassionate
4. versatile
5. amiable
6. glum
7. versatile

Page 93
Answers will vary.

Page 99
1. aunt; mother
2. kin
3. uncle; father
4. kittens
NICK

Page 105
1. scurry
2. trudge
3. lurch
4. linger
5. rummage
A STREAM

Page 111
Across
2. supervisor
6. transaction
7. inventory
8. spend
Down
1. dollar
3. receipt
4. franchise
5. store

Page 117
1. C
2. A
3. D
4. B
5. E

Page 123
1. glare
2. glimpse
3. scrutinize
4. scan
5. gaze
6. glower
7. inspect
8. glance

34. **attest**　　　attest: to swear something is true
35. **testimony**　　testimony: a statement given by a witness
36. **assert**　　　assert: to state something as being true
37. **utter**　　　　utter: to speak or make a sound
38. **reiterate**　　reiterate: to repeat something
39. **rebuke**　　　rebuke: to scold
40. **candid**　　　candid: honest and open
41. **decathlon**　　decathlon: a ten-event track competition
42. **marathon**　　marathon: a long race
43. **hurdle**　　　hurdle: a small fence that you jump over
44. **torch**　　　　torch: a flaming light that you carry
45. **ceremony**　　ceremony: a formal event
46. **minimum**　　minimum: the smallest amount possible
47. **horde**　　　　horde: a large, noisy group
48. **paltry**　　　paltry: small or worthless
49. **maximum**　　maximum: the largest amount possible
50. **abundance**　　abundance: a very large quantity of something
51. **overwhelm**　　overwhelm: to have a very strong effect
52. **appalling**　　appalling: horrifying or shocking
53. **intimidate**　　intimidate: to make someone afraid
54. **elated**　　　elated: pleased and excited
55. **grateful**　　grateful: appreciative and thankful
56. **scorching**　　scorching: very, very hot
57. **tropical**　　tropical: to be like the hot tropics
58. **temperate**　　temperate: neither too hot nor too cold
59. **torrent**　　　torrent: a fast rush of liquid
60. **frigid**　　　frigid: very, very cold
61. **extraterrestrial**　extraterrestrial: coming from outer space
62. **extraordinary**　extraordinary: very unusual
63. **extracurricular**　extracurricular: outside of school
64. **extravagant**　extravagant: very high in price
65. **extrovert**　　extrovert: an outgoing and talkative person
66. **compassionate**　compassionate: sympathetic

(Continued on page 129)

Index